Celebrate Success

How to be a successful working mum without the guilt

Gill Donnell MBE

www.successfulwomen.training

enquiries@successfulwomen.training

CONTENTS

ACKNOWLEDGMENTS

This book is dedicated to my two gorgeous girls, Drama and Crisis – sorry, Emily and Holly – who have inspired me to write down just some of the humorous episodes from our lives while we've travelled along the bumpy road as the single, working mum and her long-suffering children. We have had, and continue to have, lots of fun, and I hope they will find this advice of use to them as they begin their adult lives (far too soon for my liking!).

To my wonderful husband, Graham: thank you for continuing to support me in everything I do, despite my sometimes-unusual ideas and obsession with shoes. This is also for my brilliant stepsons, Ben and Dan, who are on their way to fulfilling their potential and making us very proud.

Thanks to my editor, Sarah Harrison, for her patience, and to Dani Dixon for the lovely design work.

Finally, without my mum and dad, and their unwavering support and encouragement throughout my life, I certainly would not have unlocked my true potential (nor managed childcare), so thank you to them for their belief in me.

ABOUT THE BOOK

As a consequence of my own 'light-bulb' moment many years ago, when I first discovered the benefits of single-gender training, unheard of in the organisation in which I worked at that time (a police force), I have developed a passion for widening access to women's personal-development training.

I should probably explain that I attended the first course of its kind, dedicated to developing senior *women* in the police. Prior to this, because men were (and still are) heavily in the majority as uniformed police officers, most training courses were single-gender by default, given there were usually only men on them!

Since taking part in that course, I have introduced personal-development programmes, training and networking opportunities to hundreds of women, and many men, across numerous organisations.

I have spent almost 15 years watching, in particular, these women discover for themselves the benefits of personal development; not only to their lives, but also to the lives of those around them. I have witnessed a huge increase in the number of women putting themselves forward for promotion, or challenging themselves to try new roles, stepping out of their comfort zones for the first time and *succeeding*.

Having concluded my 30-year police career, the last 13 years of which were as a working mother, it made sense to continue spreading the word and encouraging even more women to access their untapped potential. If you have never considered thinking of your life in this way, *Celebr8*® *Success* will help begin the process. It represents an easy-to-remember acronym, which provides a framework of attitudes to adopt and steps to follow to ensure you learn to celebrate your many achievements on the way to personal success.

If you are already on your way to fulfilling your potential, then congratulations, and I hope that some of these ideas will further support you on that journey.

Most importantly, the messages in this book are written so that we can continue to encourage each new generation of young women to have the confidence to try anything (within the bounds of decency), and find roles in organisations or companies that respect them and offer the opportunities that they seek. If such opportunities are simply unavailable, encourage them to have the confidence and enthusiasm to try elsewhere to unlock their potential, maybe even consider taking other paths such as starting their own business or moving to completely different sectors. Hopefully, in the longer term, we will see changes in their working lives and start to make inroads on differentials such as the gender pay gap, which currently suggests that full-time working women are being paid 15 per cent less than full-time working men.

Finally, to all of you reading this book, remember you are the best role models for your children – both girls and boys – and you deserve to celebrate your and their successes.

Happy reading.

GILL DONNELL MBE

FOREWORD

Have you ever been on a holiday – one of those relaxing, two-week, gloriously sunny breaks (pre-kids) – and suddenly seen your life with fierce clarity? You just know that, when you return home, everything is going to be better organised, more fun and far less stressful, because while you've been away, you have seen the light!

It's very similar to the feeling you get when you attend a course that addresses your personal development; the feeling that it could change your life. All of a sudden, you can see the right way to bring up your kids; how to support (or otherwise) your partner; and how to have a truly fulfilling life from that point on. Then, somehow, you get sucked back in to the pressures and demands of everyday life, and all those good intentions evaporate like last year's New Year's resolutions.

Well, this book is going to change all of that. I am going to show you how you can make those adjustments and keep going until they become a natural part of your life. I will prove that you too can achieve far more than you might think is possible, just by recognising your own strengths and achievements, developing some of those less positive qualities and changing things on a more permanent basis.

The aforementioned holiday was in fact my third honeymoon (did you say third?) in my 56th year (how did that happen?); oh, and following retirement from my 30-year career as a police officer (which went rather well on reflection, but more of that later).

Anyway, the idea to write this book was conceived on that honeymoon, and as you are reading it now, it is proof that just about anything can be achieved when you believe it enough and follow my eight steps.

The impetus for writing down my experiences comes from the many women I had the privilege of meeting while being the lead for women's development for 15 years in the organisation in which I worked. I frequently found myself being struck by the incredible personal achievements, sacrifices made and challenges faced by so many of these women. Yet the recurring themes were a lack of confidence in their own ability and staggering levels of low self-esteem in these otherwise high-achieving women.

On many occasions, the women involved held down high-pressured, management roles, and were outwardly extremely confident, yet inwardly had very little faith in their own abilities. Truth be told, I sometimes suffered in a similar way. At my retirement party, I spoke of expecting the boss to finally have sussed that I really never had a clue about what I was doing! Here I was, leaving the force as a chief superintendent (and not huge numbers of them were women) having received an MBE from Her Majesty for 'services to women in policing', yet I still had that niggling thought that I was going to be 'found out' one day!

The purpose of this story is to acknowledge that most women, at whatever level, have moments of doubt. The trick is to recognise them for what they are and have strategies for managing those times when they get in the way.

I recall Cherie Blair once saying: "I am not Superwoman. The reality of my daily life is that I am juggling a lot of balls in the air… And sometimes some of the balls get dropped."

The other common desire expressed to me was that golden vision of a work-life balance. In truth, this will be very different for each of us. For some, the balance may need to be heavily pivoted towards work to avoid too much involvement in what goes on at home. Others might seek to be the very vision of a perfect earth mother who is there at all times for her children, while still holding down a responsible job. Neither of these sounds particularly healthy or achievable to me.

Usually, however, we are seeking the balance that allows us to fulfil our 'mum work' alongside being successful in our professional lives, and that is what I am going to help you achieve.

I am passionate about women achieving their full potential and, being a mum of twin girls (more of Drama and Crisis later), have realised the importance of being the best role models for our daughters that we can be. This does not mean trying to be perfect, which so many women seem to think is expected of them – in fact, I have often said that if 'perfect' is the top of a scale, then a quarter of the way down is 'excellent' and that will do just fine. It *does* mean setting a good example to our children, and being confident and positive, but accepting that setbacks may happen on life's journey. This approach is more likely to give us the resilience to better deal with challenging life experiences that have the ability to derail us without this kind of preparation.

I am also stepmother to two boys, so while I will talk a lot about unlocking the potential of women and girls, this is as important for men as it is women. My personal experience of working for 30 years in a male-dominated organisation has, however, given me more of a focus on making sure women push a little harder on that glass ceiling.

This book's aim, therefore, is to help those of you who work (whether paid or unpaid) and have children or other caring responsibilities, and want to be successful at what you do, while being happy for as much of the time as possible. Oh, and if you have spent some time as a single mum, like me, and worked your way through a few marriages (I call my children's father my 'present ex-husband' to keep my current husband on his toes), then it may have extra resonance for you.

I am now going to walk you through eight steps that will help you to be successful both at work and at home, without being dragged down too much by that female albatross: guilt.

Each chapter offers more detail about these strategies and is littered with personal, real-life examples of my own to lighten the mood, but also to demonstrate some of the realities that many of us face. At the end of each chapter, I will share with you what I call *success snippets*, so you can practise the strategies and make long-term changes to turn you into that successful working mum without the guilt.

I hope you find the book enjoyable, beneficial and a long-lasting friend to guide you through the balancing act that is your personal life and work.

CHAPTER 1

Confidence and self-esteem

"No one can make you feel inferior without your consent" –
Eleanor Roosevelt

Lack of confidence and the linked psychological concept of low self-esteem are probably the two most common areas of complaint when women are asked what, if anything, is holding them back from living their life as they want.

Interestingly, male and female managers regularly raise these same issues when they talk to me about their desire to help female staff develop, seek progression or improve their ability to sell themselves in order to get the recognition that they deserve.

Confidence

What is it that makes so many of us doubt ourselves on such a regular basis?

I mentioned earlier how – even after 30 years' service, reaching a senior level in a male-dominated environment and being awarded an MBE – I thought that one day 'they' would catch me out.

It transpires that this feeling is not as unusual as you might imagine (let's be honest; we usually believe no one else shares our thoughts and insecurities). In fact, this negative way of thinking has been referred to as a psychological phenomenon known as the Impostor Syndrome, which can be defined as: The psychological experience of believing that one's accomplishments came about not through genuine ability, but as a result of having been lucky, having worked harder than others, or having manipulated other people's impressions.

Many will find it surprising to discover that even successful women who are CEOs of FTSE 100 companies admit to having moments of self-doubt. If women who have achieved that level of success can admit to such feelings, then what's to stop the rest of us from facing up to these fears and taking steps to tackle them?

Some researchers believe that low self-confidence in women is due to activity in the areas of our brains that take account of emotional responses, with these areas going on red alert when we receive negative feedback. Also, the impact on us can be much greater when we are subjected to hormonal changes. As a result, we may well pick up every emotional nuance that we sense around us, particularly just before the start of a menstrual cycle, often resulting in heightened emotional states and lower resilience when being presented with even the most constructive of criticism.

Additionally, many scientists agree that at least half of your personality comes from your genes, with the remainder being shaped by life experiences. If, therefore, you were regularly put down as a child, this message is likely to have become embedded in your brain circuitry, and be very difficult to shake off in later life. Certainly, women will often – by pure instinct and then subsequently through force of habit – focus their efforts and energies on the care and feelings of others, rather than themselves, so the devotion that is necessary to ensure our own development is taken care of does not come easily.

We all have a confident person locked inside us; we just need to find a way to let her out.

I haven't always been someone who can confidently give presentations to more than 200 people, of course, but when you have experienced running through a town centre, dressed in a tight serge skirt and heels, hanging onto your handbag (the uniform of the Eighties!) while chasing a robber and trying to speak on the radio to get assistance, it can certainly give the impression that you are a very confident person.

I will also always remember the first day I left the safety of the police station on my own, and the gentleman who was heading straight for me with no idea of how nervous I felt. I was imagining all the potential terrifying scenarios that might result from our encounter, as he approached me with such a harassed look on his face.

"At last! Officer, can you help me?"

"Of course, Sir. How can I assist?" I said, in best training-school voice, with that quizzical, confident expression on my face.

"Where is the nearest Barclays Bank?" Phew – I survived!

I had no choice, back then, but to at least *appear* to be a calm, confident swan, gliding across the surface, even though I was paddling with fury underneath. Over time, this developed into true confidence.

One of the best ways to overcome a lack of confidence is to face that fear and tackle it head on. I had little alternative when I became a police officer than to adopt an air of self-confidence. One of the main success factors for a police officer is to make sure you instill in members of the public the confidence that you can protect and serve them in whatever role you are taking on at that time.

This is the key to achieving true self-confidence: take responsibility for making the changes in your life and find the time to practise, practise and practise more.

Start small; pick something you want to be able to do well, and practise that skill. Maybe it is developing the ability to deliver a presentation in front of your team, or finding the confidence to tell your sister that you really don't want to spend yet another Christmas with her. (I confess that this has never been a particular problem for me, as I am an only child.) Practise how you will deliver your message; how you will be assertive in that conversation and, after a while, your confidence will grow.

Of course, it's probably not possible to beat the world record for the 100-metre sprint just by practising – some things are physiological too!

A good example is learning to drive. Remember the first time you sat behind the wheel of a car and everything seemed so foreign? Yet practice and some good training usually leads to us becoming confident drivers; and so it goes with self-confidence in other areas.

Going hand in hand with this concept is the need to step out of your comfort zone. So many women I know are doing absolutely fabulous jobs, but could do so much more if it weren't for fear of failure, upsetting the status quo or simply a lack of confidence in their abilities, which stops them applying for promotion or even just doing something different. Now is the time to practise pushing yourself. Take an evening class in something you know nothing about; join that new club; learn a new language. These simple steps will lead to you experimenting more in your life and expanding your horizons.

Another tip is to smile. It's amazing how effective a simple action like smiling can be, and how positive it will make you feel. Smile as you walk down the street and observe the reactions that you get. Practise the smile in a mirror first, making sure you are smiling with your eyes. (If this is not something you do regularly, definitely practise first; it can be rather frightening if the result is a manic-looking grimace that has the local armed-response team called out as you walk down the high street grinning inanely at everyone you pass.)

Finally, spend time with people who appreciate you and will tell you so. Read more on this in the chapter on Energy and enthusiasm.

One of the greatest impacts on my professional self-confidence was the belief in me expressed frequently by an old boss. (I must clarify that 'old' in this context means approximately 14 years ago, as opposed to him being long in the tooth.) It was around the time when I was starting to enter the world of senior management. It transpired that this was somewhat removed from working as a busy detective inspector where the focus, up to then, had been on locking up the bad guys. Now, life seemed to be much more about performance at strategic meetings and leading a more diverse and larger team of people.

My line manager had clearly spotted the potential in me to climb higher in the organisation, and frequently took the opportunity to tell me how capable I was and that I could go further if I chose to. Consequently, with this unusual level of emotional intelligence, he revelled in the title 'Honorary Girlie'; this approach being rather a novelty in the police service of the late Nineties.

When you hear these sorts of positive messages

on a regular basis, you begin to recognise the strengths yourself and, subsequently, are forced to start believing in them.

If you seek success in your professional world, you need positive, supportive people around you; not negative, critical voices and, importantly, that includes your own internal voice.

At this point, I would like to credit my 'current' husband and his unfailing belief in me that, apart from anything else, has resulted in me having the confidence to write this book.

Self-esteem

Even the most confident people can suffer from a loss of self-esteem, which may be caused by individual life events. Divorce, bereavement or other similar life-changing circumstances can leave us feeling vulnerable and lacking in belief in our abilities.

Sadly, I have considerable experience of supporting women with desperately low self-worth as a sole consequence of the behaviour of their partners. Emotional abuse on such a scale needs to be recognised, acknowledged as unacceptable and, when safe to do so, tackled by those of us who can bring some influence to the outcome of these situations.

Lack of self-esteem and self-worth in young girls is a particular concern of mine. Having teenage daughters brings this concept into sharp relief; looking in through the eyes of my twin girls and their friends really causes me great angst at times. How can such lovely, kind, talented and bright human beings (yes, I know I'm biased, but this goes for most of their friends too) have, what appears to be, such ingrained levels of low self-esteem at times? What makes them spend so much time on social-media websites, apparently sending and seeking to receive compliments to and from each other? There are some staggering statistics and research on the internet, including one piece stating that teenage girls who have negative views of themselves are four times more likely to take part in activities that they end up regretting later in life.

The personal-care company Dove has a fantastic mission to help the next generation of women develop a positive relationship with the way they look, helping them to raise their self-esteem and realise their full potential. Its research has shown that six out of ten girls are so concerned with the way they look that they actually opt out of participating fully in daily life; from going swimming and playing sports to going to school or even offering their opinions.

In order to start to tackle low self-esteem, we had better fully understand the concept. I like the theory suggesting that self-esteem is the result of adding self-confidence and self-respect together. Whatever our take on this psychological term, it is undoubtedly a crucial factor in our ability to achieve success and happiness in our lives.

Recognising that our position on the metaphorical scale can move up or down at times, depending on personal circumstances, how do we make changes to our levels of self-esteem for the better?

If you have a low level of self-esteem, you will usually see yourself in a negative light, focusing on your weaknesses and any mistakes you have made. Conversely, if you have a high level of self-esteem, you will see yourself in a positive light most of the time. The latter can be of great help when we do suffer adverse consequences in our lives, whether it is through such events as divorce or bereavement, or simply through making a mistake in our personal or professional lives. High self-esteem can act as a buffer and allow us to bounce back more quickly than if we had lower self-esteem.

So, start by becoming aware of all those throwaway comments you make about yourself, whether they are articulated out loud or simply played out in your head:

"If only I had different hair/eyes/hips."

"I am so bad at…"

"I can't do…"

Acknowledge that you are making these judgements and do something about them; appreciate another aspect of yourself or turn that negative belief into a positive one:

"I do have good teeth/legs/hands."

"I am getting better at…"

"I can do my very best."

Again, when it comes to young women and their body image, be aware of how you usually talk about your body in front of your daughter and stop those negative comments. Research has shown that 93 per cent of American women at college engaged in what has been called 'fat talk' with their friends:

"I really shouldn't be eating this…"

"This dress makes me look fat."

"Do my hips look big in this?"

Interestingly, I have often discussed with women similar concerns about their daughters' lack of self-esteem, but somehow they don't recognise the connection with their own self-image and self-talk.

The reality is that if you suffer from low confidence and self-esteem, you could be affecting your children too. Be kind to yourself, practise saying positive things about yourself, make a point of smiling at yourself in the mirror, and pick out positive attributes every day. Preferably, write them on a sticky note and put it where you can see it.

Start to act in a positive way, saying positive things about yourself and your personality out loud. The more often you say these things, the more likely you are to believe them. (There's that practice thing again!)

It is inevitable that the more you speak to your children in a positive way, the more benefit this will have on them. Ensure that your children hear language and comments that reassure them that there is much more to life than appearances.

So, make that initial move towards success; increase your confidence and self-esteem by stepping out of your comfort zone and doing something new. You can do it; you just have to take that first positive step.

Success snippet: Be positive about yourself and others.

CHAPTER 2

Excellence; not perfection

"If I cannot do great things, I can do small things in a great way" – Martin Luther King Jr

What is it about the fairer sex that often makes it so difficult for us to ask for help? It's almost as uncommon as a man asking for directions. My advice? Delegate as much as you can and do not get into the no-win position of playing the martyr. You will not be rewarded at the pearly gates because you did one more chore, cooked one more meal, or washed and ironed one more load of laundry.

So, please, stop trying to be the perfect wife, mother or lover – trust me, excellence is far easier to achieve than perfection!

I frequently hear friends bemoaning the amount of time it takes to do all those essential chores after their full day at work, yet they seem astonished when I suggest they might invest some of that hard-earned cash in a cleaner, gardener or – my own particular favourite – an ironing fairy.

There seem to be all manner of reasons why this 'women's work' cannot be franchised out. Surprisingly, the most common unspoken reason is that it will not be done as well as they would do it themselves. That may well be true, but is the rest of the family really going to be aghast if the shower screen has a few smudges? Will they even notice if the vacuum cleaner isn't pushed around as regularly? Of course, if they *do* want to live in an immaculate house and have cordon bleu meals, they will need to take an active role in achieving that.

I am fascinated by the conditioning that forces so many women to believe that somehow they are not good wives, partners and mothers if they do not perform *all* of those 'female' tasks themselves. Some also believe that seeking help somehow undermines their independence and ability to cope. I understand, having worked very hard at bringing up my girls without their father, that we need to tell ourselves we can cope in order to get through some of those difficult times. I am well aware, however, that I could not have achieved success in my professional life without the unfailing support of my parents – to the extent that I bought a house across the road from them (although I am not sure my father was as keen as we were on that move). It is pretty essential, if you are likely to be called back to work in the middle of the night, that your dear old dad can slip in and sleep on the settee, without disturbing the little ones. Of course, I did question this when Holly asked one day: "Whose house are we sleeping at tonight?"

Back to franchising out the chores then, or rather *not* franchising them out where stereotypically female chores are concerned.

The belief of many women that they must personally fulfil their responsibilities in terms of so-called 'female' household chores does not necessarily extend to their male partners, whose responsibilities might typically be to mend cars, decorate houses, fix plumbing, and cut the grass and hedges, as well as being full-blown technical experts and work full time. My other half is the Apple genius in our household, to the extent that he demands £80 in payment every time he gets a laptop or iPad working again. The rest of the 'boys' jobs' at home are contracted out to others, with no guilt felt at all. (Except the grass cutting, but then he does have one of those ride-on mowers that we girls are not allowed anywhere near.)

Of course, when you do give up that 'perfectionist' gene and invest in help, don't fall into the trap I am most famous for: tidying up before the cleaner comes!

If you are parting with a chunk of your hard-earned cash, take some advice and find a person who is not someone you know who has fallen on hard times, or your child's friend's mother's sister from the school gate. Try to find someone with whom you can have a proper employer/employee relationship. Take up references – this relationship is meant to make your life easier – and free up your diary and headspace for more quality time with your family and friends or, best of all, for some 'me time'.

Don't turn it into the accumulation of even more guilt, as you are forced to listen to tales of woe and gossip while the ironing fairy collects your baskets of 'smalls', or end up grudgingly parting with your cash to someone who can't grasp simple instructions.

I recall spending many cappuccino conversations with a colleague who had the same unsatisfactory cleaner for years, but whom she couldn't sack because she felt so sorry for her, despite the fact that my colleague seemed to need to tidy up after her cleaner.

This feels like an appropriate time to share with you one of my favourite poems that has been doing the rounds on the internet for some years now, and is a tribute to those of us who are out and about, living our lives, rather than spending our weekends cleaning 'just in case' someone comes round to visit!

Dust if you must, but wouldn't it be better

To paint a picture or write a letter,

Bake a cake or plant a seed,

Ponder the difference between want and need?

Dust if you must, but there's not much time,

With rivers to swim and mountains to climb,

Music to hear and books to read,

Friends to cherish and life to lead.

Dust if you must, but the world's out there

With the sun in your eyes, the wind in your hair,

A flutter of snow, a shower of rain.

This day will not come around again.

Dust if you must, but bear in mind,

Old age will come and it is not kind.

And when you go – and go you must –

You, yourself, will make more dust.

– Rose Milligan (originally published in *The Lady*, 1998)

A house becomes a home when you can write 'I love you' on the furniture. Trust me, you can write *War and Peace* on the dust in our home between 'cleans'!

Of course, if you want to influence some of the younger generation, you could always replace the word 'dust' in this poem with 'check Facebook or Twitter'.

Do the quiz below to identify if you have a faulty 'perfectionist gene':

i.   Do you find yourself reloading the dishwasher after the kids have loaded it? (It won't clean properly with the knives that way up.)

ii.   Do you keep the whole of that work project to yourself, despite having to work late most nights to meet the deadline? (It would take far too long to explain how you want it done to anyone else.)

iii.   Do you check and then alter your children's homework? (You wouldn't want the teacher to think you don't care.)

iv.   Do you iron pants and socks? (I have finally stopped this one.)

v.   Do you seek perfection in all that you do? (And do you understand why?)

I do realise that some of you may not suffer from this angst, and consequently have a healthy relationship with the sharing of tasks, such as cooking, cleaning, washing and so on. However, if you answered yes to most or all of these questions, it's useful to try to understand why it is so important for you to want to be perfect.

Perfection for you could be on a sliding scale, with obsessive-compulsive disorder at one end and the inability to go to bed without wiping down the cleared kitchen surfaces somewhere towards the other end. (Okay, I just find it *difficult* to sleep if I haven't wiped them down with a brief spray of bleach, and I don't think that's OCD.)

It is generally accepted that women are more likely to strive to achieve perfection than men in similar situations. The media plays a big part in this pressure, flooding us with unrealistic expectations at every opportunity, in particular, impacting disproportionately on the younger generation. The most popular magazines, aimed at women and men, tend to feature women with bodies that are unattainable to the average woman, and depictions of success and happiness reliant on one's ability to snap up a suitable partner. I guarantee that of the magazines aimed at female readers on sale in your local newsagent, around three quarters will have covers featuring articles on diets or some other way to change your physical appearance. We are now starting to see more diversity in the appearances of many of the women given prominent roles in the visual media, with the 'best parts' in television and films not just featuring those who are young and pretty – but, please, don't get me started on the depiction of female characters in popular video games!

Our upbringing can also have a great impact on in-built personal expectations and unrealistic standard setting. This type of influence, much like the 'body talk' in the previous chapter, is often transferred from generation to generation. Although some inherited traits will be of great benefit to us in our professional lives, such as a 'strong work ethic' or an 'ability to work well under pressure', as with anything, it is the extremes that can lead to an unhealthy outcome, such as feeling it is necessary to work a 60-70-hour week to become successful.

For many years I observed numerous talented women refusing to even consider putting themselves forward for promotion or to seek a different role due to their belief that they did not have all of the requisite skills for the position. This may seem sensible and straightforward, but the reality is that men often do not set themselves such high expectations in terms of their suitability for a role.

So, how does that play out in the workplace? If a job advertisement lists six required skills from candidates, many women look at the list, identify that they possess five but are not as strong on the sixth and, as a result, make a decision to not even take the first step and apply for the job. Most men, on the other hand, will not be so particular; they may well take a look at those requirements, count off perhaps three attributes, but decide it is worth 'giving it a punt'. So, what is the outcome? As my (male) Chief Constable would say: "The 'chancer' gets the job!"

This example is not intended to put down men who adopt this approach, but to celebrate the fact that they are prepared to sell themselves and give it a go. So many women, on the other hand, miss those opportunities, because they have become entrenched in their need for perfection and believe that they must fulfil each criterion. As I said earlier, excellence will do just fine.

Many of my coaching conversations with women prior to job interviews concentrate on the need to sell themselves; something that seems to be surprisingly difficult for so many, considering the perfectionist mindset that they clearly inhabit. It is so important to believe a positive commercial about yourself, and certainly not be tempted to bring up any negatives in interviews. In my experience, these opinions are unlikely to be accurate anyway, and by following my advice, you won't suddenly turn into an arrogant hot-favourite for *The Apprentice*. Modesty, however, is unlikely to get you that dream job; you need to recognise your achievements, be proud of them and then celebrate them. More of that in the final chapter.

If you are already in a leadership position at work and able to delegate to colleagues or more junior staff, but find it very difficult because of your need to deliver perfection, consider some of the advantages of creating such a situation.

Many managers are often shocked when we

discuss this topic in coaching, as the recognition dawns on them that they are holding others back by not allowing them to take on work. How are people going to learn and grow if they are not given the opportunity to take on some of those tasks? Of course, that doesn't mean dumping a whole load of work, walking away without offering any advice, and then demanding the resultant output the following day. A good leader is one who leads a happy, productive team, in whom they have confidence, and who has the time to support and coach to achieve results; not one who is shut in their office, surrounded by piles of work, harassed and under pressure with never enough time to listen to their staff.

A personal-development concept that I love is that of 'failing brilliantly'. The argument here is that we cannot develop, learn and succeed (unless we are incredibly lucky) without failing at some point and we should embrace that part of the process. As young children, we have no reticence about doing things wrong, but as we get older inhibitions appear and we become embarrassed if we make mistakes, feeling awkward when events don't happen as we think they should and before we know where we are, the simplest of errors becomes a negative failure.

Yet even the most successful people have invariably failed or had setbacks from which they have clearly learned. A newspaper editor supposedly sacked Walt Disney because he lacked imagination and had no good ideas.

Winston Churchill spent much of the Thirties in a political wilderness until becoming Prime Minister at the age of 62. One of my favourite quotes of his regarding failure starts off Chapter 4 of this book: "Success consists of going from failure to failure without loss of enthusiasm."

The subject of striving for perfection has come up in education too. A recently published *The Good Schools Guide* has suggested that children need to learn to deal with failure in order to be able to cope with setbacks later in life. "If we drive our children to define themselves only by success, how will they deal with the inevitable setbacks that come with adulthood?" the guide asks. "Are we creating a generation who won't have a go at something new for fear of failing?" Helen Fraser, the chief executive of the Girls' Day School Trust said: "We need to ensure that their education helps them to become resilient, to encourage them to not be afraid to take risks and to be confident."

So, embrace excellence, or even less than excellence on occasions, and don't push yourself to achieve excessively high standards, whether set by yourself or others around you. I was never one to worry about that last-minute "Mum, we need to take a cake into school tomorrow; will you make one?" If such obstacles trouble you, can I encourage you to sneak off to the 24-hour supermarket, buy a 'home-made' cake and throw a bit of icing sugar around? Perfect!

Oh, and to prove this sentiment extends into business, there is a poster at the Facebook head office that says: 'Done is better than perfect'.

Success snippet: Ask for help — and then take it!

GILL DONNELL MBE

CHAPTER 3

Lead and be authentic

"When the best leader's work is done, the people say we did it ourselves" – Lao Tzu

Given that my passion is to do all I can to support women in reaching their full potential, at least one of these chapters has to be dedicated to leadership in the workplace.

That doesn't mean that if you are content in your role at work you should skip straight to the next chapter. All of us are leaders at times, particularly those of us who are mothers, depending perhaps on the attitudes of others in the house towards our role. I have, on occasions, had to remind certain young people in our house who the adults are. Consequently, there is a requirement for some of us to make a conscious effort to behave like an adult most of the time; not something I always find terribly easy. According to some of my girls' friends, I am a 'ledge' which, I have had explained to me, is short for legend, and apparently is excruciatingly embarrassing for my girls. Still, as I have frequently explained, the purpose of being a parent is to embarrass your children as often as possible.

So far I have talked about a number of female traits that, in excess, could have a negative impact on women as individuals. In this chapter, I will emphasise the positive side of a typically female leadership style.

So, what are women typically good at? Caring for people, listening with empathy, seeking the views of others, multitasking and, hopefully now, asking for help. These are just a few well-known female strengths that can be successfully transferred into the workplace. Too often I have talked to women who will not push themselves forward because, in their eyes, they have no relevant skills. As I said in the previous chapter, don't wait for every box to be ticked; instead, look at the transferable skills you have, and work out how they fit into your organisation.

A lot of recent research recognises that women can teach men a lot about being a successful leader, with the mainly macho style of transactional 'do as I say' leadership having less and less relevance in today's workplace. More emphasis is now being placed upon those emotional qualities that have been identified as making leaders more effective. In the mid Nineties, the term 'emotional intelligence' was brought to a wider audience, and five components were identified that, added together, could drive outstanding performance at work: self-awareness, self-regulation, motivation, empathy and social skills. In many business surveys, women score more highly than men in a number of these areas, with self-awareness and empathy usually topping those lists. At last, we can begin to see the positives in some of those 'female' qualities we examined in earlier chapters.

If you still require some persuasion that you have the right skills, do a skills audit. Consider something like a brainstorm of the major projects you have been involved in at work, then think in detail of the actions you needed to take and skills you utilised to complete your role in the project. Make a list, a physical list that you can see and add to, of your strengths in terms of these professional qualities, but be creative and look across your entire life and at your achievements, as well as at your accomplishments at work. You will find plenty of advice and support on the internet to help you complete this.

If you already have a particular plan to move jobs or retrain, then make another list of the skills you will need in order to move roles or successfully perform the new role, remembering, of course, that this list is not then to be used to stop you applying for jobs based on specific criteria.

Perhaps you have been involved in running the school PTA and have therefore had to use good organisational, event–planning or fundraising skills. You may have had to guide others, and consequently discovered you are a good negotiator and can successfully influence other people. This type of audit helps you identify these qualities, and can give you far more confidence and belief in your own abilities, both at work and at home.

Assuming, then, that you accept my premise that you might well have the necessary skills to become a successful leader after all, what are the important qualities needed to achieve this?

I have always been a great believer in demonstrating authenticity at work, and by that I mean bringing the real you into the workplace and not 'acting the part'. Too often, I have watched female colleagues acting like 'one of the boys' in an effort to be accepted; a far more common trait in male-dominated organisations, such as the police and fire services. While I understand the need to fit in, especially if you are the only woman on a shift and at risk of isolation for being 'different', in my experience this type of response is not helpful when you are trying to be effective. As we have already discussed, women tend to be hardwired to seek cooperation and collaboration; they are more likely to want to find solutions that benefit the majority, and certainly take members of the team along with them. If you believe that these traits won't be appreciated in your group, and seek to mask them by acting differently, then there is a good chance this will start affecting you at home, as the dissonance between these two styles (assuming you act in a more traditional way at home) begins to have an impact.

If this rings true with you, I recommend you stop acting like a bloke and start behaving authentically. Be true to yourself and make sure that what you do is in line with your values. This may take more courage for some than others, but ultimately it will have a more beneficial long-term effect on you and your career. If you are having difficulty identifying what leadership means for you, then have a look around at those female leaders whom you admire or who inspire you.

How do they work with others; what makes them successful; and what is it about them that inspires you? If necessary, look for a mentor to help you with your personal development. You will find more on this in Chapter 6.

One of the most satisfying aspects of *my* career has been the ability to 'grow' people, watching members of my team develop and flourish, by taking the time to help, guide and offer advice, and being there to listen to them. It's essential to tell people when they have done well – remember my old boss doing that for me? Something that simple can reap such great rewards, so do make the time to go out and talk to others; find out what they are doing; be interested; and tell them if they have done well. Don't pay lip service to this or adopt a 'Young Mr. Grace'– "You've all done very well" attitude (for those of you who have absolutely no idea what I am talking about, look up 'Young Mr. Grace' in *Are You Being Served?* on YouTube).

Behaving in this way is far more likely to create an atmosphere where your team can be honest with you. There have been many occasions when I have had what I thought were great ideas, but not being a 'completer' or a 'finisher' meant that I invariably had to rely on others to follow projects through, while I started on the next 'great idea'. It was not unusual for me to announce my latest suggestion at the Monday-morning team meeting, only to find my colleagues suggesting we should consider discussing things in a little more detail before moving on to the next agenda item. Of course, what that really meant was: "Hold on boss; don't forget the rest of us have got to put these crazy ideas into practice." It was a good check for me and made sure we all understood the consequences of the latest plan. I didn't take this challenging the wrong way, but rather recognised it as being good communication between the members of a high-performing team. As an authentic leader you should speak the truth and, while it may require personal courage at times, it also means being able to listen to others and hearing constructive criticism.

I recall an appraisal meeting with a male member of staff many years ago. He had been transferred to my team in an effort to assist in the development of his communication skills, and there I was giving authentic comments and offering words of encouragement, or so I thought. We moved on to the 360-degree feedback that ensured I was properly evaluating my own performance. Well, did I get that and then some? He stated that I was one of the most difficult people he had ever worked for and began giving me examples of why he felt that way. To be honest, I can't recall how I dealt with the meeting after this point, but I do know that his words have stuck with me ever since. Removing much of the emotion that he felt, it became clear to me that I did not have a particularly expressionless face – no surprise to my family members here. Indeed, when dealing with him in a number of situations, the expression on my face had clearly conflicted with the message I was giving. Not terribly authentic then.

Of course, that doesn't mean that we need to hurt people in our search for authenticity, but that example reinforced my need to make sure my face didn't show disappointment in, or sometimes a complete lack of tolerance of, others. You'd probably have to ask my husband how well I am succeeding in that life lesson. I do know, however, that one of my daughters has inherited this characteristic and, trust me, it tends to not sit well on the face of a 15-year-old.

So, while I am not keen on focusing on the concept of weaknesses, it helps us all as leaders to recognise into what areas we could put a little more effort. Don't be afraid to ask for help, not just at home, but at work too. If your organisation has a coaching and/or mentoring scheme, find out how you can get involved. If it doesn't, consider seeking help from your line manager. In my experience, one of the greatest compliments is when someone asks to benefit from your knowledge and experience.

Good leaders lead from their heart and are not afraid to show their vulnerability. Many people believe that vulnerability in a leader is a weakness, but

I would like to counter that argument. (Actually, I have found that a lot of men believe vulnerability full stop is a weakness, but that is probably a whole different book.)

There does need to be some clarity here, because I am not talking about letting out all of your emotions in front of your team. If you are the boss, you need to demonstrate courage and professionalism, but that doesn't mean you can't have one or two close confidantes at work to support you if things happen to be really tough, either at home or at work.

The breakdown of my second marriage took place at the time when I was starting that climb up the ladder into senior management. My ex and I were both police officers, although not in the same area. I am still quite proud of the fact that I only ever took one day off to indulge myself in that unhappiness. As a consequence, however, there were times when the challenges became very overwhelming, and a couple of close friends at work helped me keep things on track. Of course, the black humour that emergency-service workers often adopt in difficult times helped as well.

I recall a colleague commenting on how much weight I had lost and asking how I had managed to achieve it. My reply? "It's not difficult when your husband's walked out, but I probably wouldn't recommend that to everyone." Poor thing; she had no idea, but it did make me smile, and for a number of years we recounted that story when the conversations in the office turned to weight!

No, I am talking about the vulnerability that comes with accepting you don't have all the answers, or that sometimes you make mistakes and – for the sake of repetition – letting go of the need to be perfect. Put simply, being human; not a way in which all leaders seem to naturally behave, in my experience. A good example of this collaborative approach concerns South West Airlines, now one of the most successful airlines in America. In its early days, the company faced having to sell one of its four aeroplanes, as it could not continue to run them all efficiently. The boss chose to gather all of the staff together and ask for help in tackling the situation. The resultant collaboration of two sets of employees changed the turnaround time at destinations from one hour to ten minutes, allowing them to not only continue as a company, but also become (and still be to this day) an industry leader in quick turnarounds. So, work together with your team and discover for yourself, as I did, that many of the best ideas come from those on the shop floor.

I want to say something here about being a successful leader and a successful mother. I won't be discussing guilt in this chapter, as that comes later, but I guarantee that you can be both (albeit not

always at the same time in terms of success).
Currently, there is a growing concern being expressed
that many young women are stepping away from
leadership roles, despite all the efforts of their
grandmothers and mothers to make their path easier
to negotiate. To some, these women are letting down
all those who preceded them, and certainly the
number of women on executive boards is not rising
anywhere near as much as has previously been
predicted. Why is this the case? Is it the raised media
expectations for women generally, never mind for
those who put themselves in a position of public
leadership?

I heard one of the first women to hold the rank
of chief constable, speak at a conference back in the
late Nineties. A national newspaper that wanted to
write an article about her in her new job had
approached her, and what picture did they want to
accompany it? A shot of her in full uniform in the
office? Or perhaps an image of her walking the streets
with her officers? No, they wanted a picture of her
washing up in her Marigolds! Funny, I don't recall
seeing pictures in the news of male chief constables
or recently appointed CEOs repairing the lawn
mower.

Could it be that more young women believe that
perfection is necessary in order for women to be
successful in leadership positions, or the old argument

that women have to work twice as hard to have the same impact still stands?

There are many reasons at play for not wanting to take up leadership roles, but one that particularly concerns me is the apparent instinct not to push forward because of the potential problems such a role might bring when trying to achieve a comfortable work/life balance. I recall a coaching conversation with a younger colleague who was considering studying for the examination necessary to be promoted to the rank of inspector in the police service. (I should add that passing the examination is not the only requirement to secure the promotion.) During our conversation, she talked about her desire to start a family at some point, and the difficulties this would inevitably bring should she be trying to study or even trying to secure a new job further down the line. To my mind, she was already writing herself out of any future promotions before even reaching the stage of 'trying for a baby'. This took no account of how long it might take to actually fall pregnant, never mind coming to that decision with her partner in the first place. In reality, she was considering putting a hold on her career (or even a full stop) on the basis of what could happen in the future and how difficult it might or might not turn out to be.

My advice to her and others? Take opportunities as they arise and don't make career decisions on what may happen in the future. This automatically builds a barrier to your career and can leave you too far behind the curve later in life when your choices might be more limited. As I said to my young colleague, if you were to begin studying for the examination, you could – if necessary – stop. If you pass the exam, you could choose to take it no further, but if you carried on as though it was your goal right now (we had ascertained it was a future goal), then you might actually achieve it before hearing the sound of any little feet.

I had my girls at the age of 40. This doesn't necessarily mean I would recommend waiting that long, but as I continued with my career, I found that senior positions inevitably allowed me to have more flexibility on how I worked and, of course, it meant I could be a positive role model to others coming up behind me. But more of that later.

I hope that you can see how many of these typical female qualities can truly work for you in positions of leadership. Grab hold of every opportunity and seize the day.

Success snippet: Don't put off until tomorrow what you can do today.

CHAPTER 4

Energy and enthusiasm

"Success consists of going from failure to failure without loss of enthusiasm" – Winston Churchill

This chapter is about finding new ways to achieve happiness and be successful, and consequently identifies people whom it might be worth avoiding and situations to steer clear of if you want to live your life to the full.

Begin by ensuring that you avoid excessive exposure to the Dementors in your life. You know the type of person (I call them Dementors, as in *Harry Potter*) – the individuals you come across who seem to instantly drain all the happiness out of the world.

There's the friend who years ago was such fun when you worked together, but now seems to get all her enjoyment from sucking the joy out of everyone else's lives. She calls you to meet for coffee, apparently to hear about your new job, husband or planned holiday, but then spends three lattes telling you how no one appreciates her at work, her partner doesn't help her, none of her friends call anymore, and so on – never once asking about your life. Oh, and you'll probably have paid for the lattes too!

There's also the colleague in the office who spends more time moaning about the boss than actually doing any work.

The sad reality is that if you have too many people like this in your life, their negativity is going to rub off on you. It's very difficult to set yourself challenging goals, think yourself into the right mindset to apply for that new job, or just have fun in your everyday life when there's a negative moaner at your shoulder, pulling you down with them.

Look at the people around you; are they drains who dash the fun out of life, or are they enthusiastic people, radiating success, who make you smile and whom you want to be around?

Enthusiasm is contagious. If you surround yourself with enthusiastic people, things will start to happen; you'll feel able to finish that project, believe that you are good enough to apply for that job, and generally have the energy to do so much more. Believe me – success attracts success.

I have a friend named Annie, fondly known as 'my little friend', because there is quite a difference between us on the vertical scale. I do not know a more kind, selfless, happy and enthusiastic person, and her enthusiasm for life rubs off on me quite regularly. We often work together on various projects, and there have been times when the challenges of leaving my house very early with everything I need, as well as making sure that others are in order, packed and ready for school/work and so on, have caused me to feel just a little overwhelmed.

Of course, as we now know, this may sometimes be reflected in the expression on my face, but after 10 minutes in Annie's company, the whole world feels different. She'll tell me how she was a bit late because she pulled her car over and got out to look at the beautiful rainbow across the fields, when all I had noticed that morning were the enormous puddles I was having to navigate out of our village.

I listen to her telling me about paddling in the sea with her grandchild, getting soaking wet and her best shoes covered in sand, with no hint of regret. I have watched her skip across the lovely expanse of grass in front of the venue where we were working, because she just had to; it was somehow calling to her.

The effect of this, apart from cheering me up immensely, is that I make a promise to myself to keep up my plans to adopt a more enthusiastic approach to life. It works, too. One of my car journeys takes me down a busy A road at a relatively high level, offering a wonderful, almost bird's-eye view of the surrounding countryside. I regularly look at these vistas, unlike many who I'm sure drive on, engrossed in their thoughts or the radio, not actually noticing what is around them. I look and appreciate how fortunate I am to have such a stunning commute. If you need a top-up of enthusiasm, I recommend being more aware of your surroundings. Even among the chaos and alongside the dramas, we are all exposed to natural beauty at one point or another – make sure you pause to absorb it. (But please continue to concentrate on the road if you are driving. I really don't want to be the cause of you driving into the car in front because you were admiring the gorgeous spring lambs in the adjacent field.)

That reminds me of an outing, in my effort to spend quality time with Drama and Crisis, that resulted in them being traumatised for quite some time. They would have been about eight years of age when I took them to a local agricultural college that had been advertising open days for visitors to see the lambs. Well, I don't think we had lived in the countryside for very long and, being a city girl at heart, all I could visualise was something out of the *Teletubbies*; cute little creatures gambolling across the picturesque fields. The reality, however, could not have been more different. Firstly, it was a very wet, cold day, and extremely muddy. I don't think at that point I had bought my pink, Paisley, 'heeled' Wellington boots, and so the girls and I were wearing most inappropriate footwear. We climbed onto the back of a trailer being pulled up the hill to the 'sheds' to see the lambs, and sat among the many other correctly attired families. Then, suddenly, we were dropped off in a huge, muddy expanse surrounded by enormous sheds housing the focus of our trip.

Well, I have never seen so much blood and gore in all my life. Unbeknown to me, the point of the exercise was to watch the lambs being born – yuck. I forget the number of times we watched staff members assisting the struggling ewes by pulling out these little, bloodied bundles of fluff, a number of whom clearly had not survived the exercise. I'm sure those of you who live and breathe country life will think this all very pathetic, but we couldn't get out of there quick enough, as yet another child squealed to its parent: "That one's not moving either; is it okay?" and a pressurised member of staff was called to help out again.

In fact, I had to change one of our routes home from school for several weeks to avoid a field of lambs, as the girls kept reliving the ordeal of our trip. To this day, my eldest won't eat lamb.

I digress – how do you spot enthusiastic people if they are not skipping across the grass? There are a number of simple characteristics to look out for:

- They usually radiate energy, and by that I mean positive energy; people turn and look when they enter a room.

- They focus on the good stuff and will talk about what they *can* do, rather than what they *can't* do. Nor are you likely to hear them use the words 'should have' or 'ought to'. You will instead hear 'want to' or 'going to'.

- They are passionate, in the sense that they have a passion for what they are doing and can rouse that enthusiasm in others.

- They usually laugh a lot; a good thing, as this can lead to the release of those feel-good endorphins, which can also temporarily relieve pain. How cool is that?

- They are usually reasonable and understanding – something I am still working on.

These, then, are the attributes to build upon if you want to be recognised as an enthusiastic person. To be able to keep this up, though, requires high levels of energy, and for that we must look after ourselves. It is not – repeat after me – *not* selfish to look after yourself. Why do they tell you to put oxygen masks on yourself before helping others on the aeroplane? Because you are no use to anyone if you cannot breathe yourself.

Re-energising is crucial to ensuring you have the ability to meet the demands in your life, but in a healthier and happier way.

I am not going to repeat the widespread advice on eating, drinking and exercising for a healthier lifestyle, particularly given that the chocolate/wine/coffee addict writing this is still trying to improve on those areas. It is more important to recognise the benefits and not strive to be extraordinarily fit and healthy overnight, as you run the risk of becoming even more overwhelmed because you have failed to meet impossible diet and exercise targets that you set yourself.

Research states that the act of exercise also releases feel-good brain chemicals (neurotransmitters and endorphins) that may ease anxiety and even depression, aside from increasing body temperature, which may have calming effects (not sure that works with hot flushes). This doesn't mean that you have to join a gym or start training for the London Marathon; simple pleasures, such as going for regular walks, can make a huge difference to your well-being, as well as your waistline.

Spend time with people who make you feel good. The simple acts of having a cup of tea, going for a walk or run, reading with your children, or laughing with your friends or partner pay huge dividends for the heart, mind, and soul, and don't usually cost very much.

The difficulty for many mothers, whether doing paid work or not, seems to be making time for themselves. Somehow, due to many of the reasons we have already discussed, the prospect of having time to re-energise seems completely alien and certainly selfish. In fact, working mums tend to feel particularly guilty at spending time on their own, as they often feel that when they are not at work, they should spend as much time as possible with their children, rather than indulging in 'me time'. This can result in those spare hours being used to catch up on a few extra household chores. Can I encourage you to not go down that route? Instead, practise, practise and practise filling time with activities that have a positive impact on your well-being. Recognise that the frazzled, stressed, overwhelmed woman you sometimes become is of no help to anyone.

I am told that many people successfully keep house plants (I am definitely not one of these people) and, when doing so, water and even feed them in the knowledge that failing to complete these actions (as I do quite regularly) will result in them shrivelling up and dying. Yet, somehow, we expect that *we* can survive without such care and attention. We, too, need fuel, and I don't just mean food and water. We need to top up those energy reserves, and one of the quickest ways to do this is to take a step off the daily treadmill and do something that makes you feel emotionally rewarded. Again, it doesn't have to cost a lot of money, although a 12-hour spa day is likely to be hugely beneficial; just a walk in the fresh air or going to the afternoon showing of that film you've been wanting to see can make a real difference. The likelihood is that you will consequently feel more refreshed and able to continue spinning your own personal plates more successfully.

So, let's look at the pros and cons of taking 'me time':

Pros:

- You will feel invigorated.

- The children get to spend more time with their father/grandparents/friends.

- You will recognise how much you enjoy your place in the family.

- Your physical and psychological well-being will be improved.

Cons:

- You will discover that they can in fact manage without you.

- The house will become a disaster area.

- You'll spend forever paying back the favour to father/grandparents/friends.

- You will realise you don't want to give it up.

There is no doubt that we are living increasingly busy lives. Busyness seems to have turned into some sort of social disease, with many people I know seemingly trying to outdo each other by saying how *very* busy they are in response to a simple "How are you?"

These frenetic mindsets are certainly the enemy of energy and enthusiasm and, given that we now have much more technology than our mothers ever had, we seem to have filled up all of those newly created spare hours with other very important 'stuff'.

So, here's a reminder of those good old-fashioned tips that can lead to a healthier and more productive life:

- Get enough sleep. Apart from anything else, the various stages of sleep are essential to allow us to make space in our brains for the next load of data.

  For someone like me, whose brain seems to be permanently too full to take any more in, sleep is vital.

- Drink water. I recently heard that a glass of water before bed can stave off heart attacks and strokes.

  This got me glugging an extra litre down (meaning I now have to get up even more in the night, which may be the reason that my brain hasn't yet made the necessary space in my mental filing cabinets!).

- Make a list of everything that needs doing. It is more beneficial to do this before you go to bed, as this is one of the most common reasons for feeling overwhelmed and being unable to sleep. Get everything down on a piece of paper or the notes page on your smartphone, and work up a plan for getting through the tasks. If you can't get to sleep because of what is going around in your head, then you can add these thoughts to your list.

- Schedule no-appointments time in your diary. This is a good way of ensuring you don't miss your 'me time', but also to avoid double booking family events with work commitments.

  I have finally let go of my pretty, hard-copy diary and succumbed to technology after missing an appointment that had not found its way into my paper diary. As a family, we now have a number of shared calendars, accessible across our smartphones, colour coded and, if necessary, with alarms, so that everyone knows what is happening at various times. As we rarely go anywhere without our phones, there is no longer an excuse for missing parents' evening or something similar. (Unless of course you happen to not set the alarm on the diary entry – oops!)

- Indulge yourself in healthy activities as much as you can. Be passionate and remember that striving towards a goal without passion is like a fire slowly running out of fuel. Get excited; this means that you will love what you are doing, and others will love being around you.

- Finally, pass your enthusiasm on to others — get out of the car and look at that rainbow.

Success snippet: Be passionate.

CHAPTER 5

Banish the guilt!

"Never regret anything, because at one time it was what you wanted" – Unknown

It seems to me that there is little point in having a book with the subtitle 'How to be a successful working mum without the guilt' and not tackle the elephant in the room head on.

I am, of course, talking about working-mum guilt and not the guilt that comes with having committed some sort of sin or done something bad to another human being. If this is the reason you have picked up this book, we should probably part company here.

No, I mean the guilt that so many women feel when juggling a variety of home and work roles.

The first thing is to accept feeling guilty as normal. According to a recent study, 96 per cent of women feel guilty at least once a day, with over half of those questioned going on to say that they had guilt feelings more than four times a day. These are emotions that can, potentially, have a destructive effect on our health never mind making us feel quite miserable at the same time. Experts have identified that women tend to internalise faults, and blame themselves when things go wrong. Men, on the other hand, will usually point the finger at external reasons for failure or mistakes. It is suggested that the reason for this difference is due to the female trait of prioritising the care of others over themselves; something that has come up in this book several times already. If women don't feel they are performing their various roles as wife, mother, daughter or friend as they (or others) believe they should, then they start to feel guilty.

If we accept that these feelings are 'normal' and undoubtedly being experienced by millions of other women around the globe, the key to combating them is to carry on and make the most of your time in whatever role you are fulfilling.

In order to reduce negative feelings, start by acknowledging that each of the roles you fulfil doesn't necessarily occur in a convenient, consecutive way. You are not mummy from 6:00–9:00am, then busy professional from 9:00am–5:00pm, daughter/friend from 5:00–6:30pm, wife and mummy again from 6:30-10:00pm, then lover from 10:00pm (if you're still awake!). Those roles happen simultaneously; you don't stop being mum when at work and, likewise, your job role may demand some of that precious time when you are at home with your family.

It's therefore important to make the home time that you *do* have, *quality* time. It's surely better to have two hours of being totally focused on and enjoying your family, with the BlackBerry turned off, rather than up to four hours trying to do everything at once, but not actually doing anything properly.

Most of us are not on-call hospital consultants or senior police officers (well, as you know, I have been the latter, but even then I was not permanently on call – unlike some male colleagues who operated as though they were). Despite our 'the world will end if I don't…' mentality, emails usually *will* wait. Similarly, if you are – as my girls like to remind me – 'from the younger generation', leave Facebook, Twitter and computer games alone for that time. Interact with your family and friends; cook a meal; play a game; maybe even go outside. It really is all about the quality, not the quantity, so when making precious time for family and significant others, make sure you are truly present. This doesn't mean that you have to do exactly what the kids demand for every minute that you are at home; they need to understand the concept of how the chores are divvied out, and take their share, but surely the world won't end if you walk away from that messy kitchen and play a few board games before bedtime, rather than be the stressed yet 'perfect' mum who has "just got far too much to do to be able to play right now." (I understand if you wish to replace board games with video or computer games, but I would still like to make a plea for old-fashioned physical interaction.)

I have known so many women, including myself on occasions, to play the martyr, overwhelmed by chores, making outstanding jobs the focus of their thoughts, and letting the precious time with loved ones pass by, all while complaining of not being able to find the right work-life balance. A useful exercise is to consider this: If today were your last day on earth, how would you choose to spend your time? I doubt it would be loading the dishwasher. (I'm well aware that these chores need to be done at some point; all I'm saying is that sometimes we need to take a step back and gain a bit of perspective.)

So, if you need to, it might be worth re-reading Chapter 2 and making sure that some of this guilt you are feeling is not as a result of you setting yourself incredibly high standards that even Mother Theresa would have difficulty attaining. Share the workload around the whole family!

I am also a strong believer in making sure that children understand why so many demands are placed upon us, as helpfully demonstrated some years ago by my dear old dad.

There I was, a single mum of twin girls aged six, lovingly nicknamed Drama and Crisis, a busy detective chief inspector – a bit like Helen Mirren in *Prime Suspect* (without the skimpy tops and short skirts) – letting my dad in to our bungalow at 8:00am to watch *Tiny Tots* with the girls before taking them to school for me. On this particular morning, the regular question: "Why can't *you* take us or collect us from school like the other mummies?" was wearing a bit thin, so I asked my dad to have a word with them.

Later on that night, my eldest daughter (by one minute, but gosh is that important) asked: "Mummy, what's a scabby flat?"

"What do you mean, sweetie?" was my confused reply.

"Joe Joe [their pet name for Grandpa] says that if you didn't go to work, we'd have to live in a scabby flat and not go on holidays – you're not going to stop working now are you?"

Working guilt banished in a nanosecond!

Mind you, this same daughter – while on one of those holidays – asked me when I was going to get a rich boyfriend, after I'd turned down her request for more ice cream through apparent lack of money.

My girls have always had a level of understanding that money and time were limited, even though I was fortunate enough to have a good job that allowed for treats and, yes, sometimes I was tempted to over-compensate by buying their happiness. Of course, now, some years down the line, they accept that if I say I will advance them pocket money or pick up that must-have mascara, they are expected to pay me back.

Looking back over the 13 years of their lives when I worked full time – up to 60 hours a week at times – despite forgetting parents' evenings, missing school plays and being late for sports' days, are those their abiding memories? No. Truthfully, they say they were proud of the fact that when they Googled my name in their IT lesson, I came top of the list of suggestions.

As for school events, I'm still reminded by Emily about the one time I took part in the mums' race when they were seven, and apparently cheated! (I think Holly might have been quite impressed, although she has never actually admitted this.)

Even though I won, they showed no pride in the outcome. My desire to win was probably something to do with the fact that I had recently discovered I was the oldest mum in the school.

"How do you know that?" was my somewhat astonished reaction.

"Oh, we asked everyone how old their mums were. You're even older than our teacher," was the casual reply.

Anyway, this 48-year-old had beaten the young mums who *did* manage to make it to the school gate, even if she had had to cheat a tad to achieve it. (If you're really interested, I only misjudged the turn, and didn't actually go around the cone halfway up the course. I'm not even sure anyone else noticed.) The best result was that the girls banned me from attending any more sports' days for fear of causing further embarrassment. It's difficult to feel guilty about not making sports' day if you have been barred!

So, what is my experience of the most common form of guilt in working mothers? Being at work rather than at home with the children.

Earning money may well be essential, but it is worth recognising the benefits that it brings to you and those around you. Be honest in acknowledging that your efforts provide for the family in terms of holidays, car, new clothes or whatever else is the case, but ensure that if the financial load is shared, your partner realises why this is important to you. Of course, it's also rather handy to have a stash of what I have been known to call 'running-away money'. This backfired recently, though, when I asked my husband about the location of funds relating to a recent policy that had matured. Apparently, it was in *his* account because it was *his* running-away money.

I have always advocated to other women who fret over the work/life juggling act, the benefits of making a list of all the positive aspects of working (or not working if that is what's making you feel guilty). Once it is complete, make sure it is put somewhere that you (and perhaps others) can see it regularly.

For example:

Pros of being a working mum:

- The ability to have a normal conversation with other adults that does not involve stamping feet and a demand for another story, song or episode of the *Tweenies*. (Replace *Tweenies* with current favourite toddler television show.)

- Getting dressed in presentable clothes and heels (preferably with matching handbag).

- Being able to walk away in the morning from

the nursery/child minder's or poor grandparents', who already look exhausted, with a big kiss and a "see you later."

- Knowing that you are being a role model and demonstrating a work ethic that your children will remember for years to come.

- Nice holidays. It's no good; they are a weakness of mine. However, my salary also ensured the mortgage was paid when there were just the three of us.

Cons of being a working mum:

- Tiredness. Oh my goodness, I'm not sure I can begin to explain the tiredness of working a 10-hour shift after being up half the night with a sick child.

- Rushing home from work to hear news from school, only to find it has already been told to Grandma, and no way in the world was it going to be repeated for my benefit.

- Reinforcing with some colleagues the value of retaining women in the workplace, particularly if you work flexibly.

- Not being on the beach or in the park for the whole of the summer holidays.

- For most people, the cost and inflexibility of

childcare.

I cannot stress enough the benefits of being a good role model to your children, and this is not just about setting an example to your daughters. Should your son ultimately settle down with a woman, would you expect her to be an equal partner? However, as in so many other areas of our lives, the guilt pedlars often come along and start criticising our efforts to bring up our children. Don't listen; there is no single right way to raise your offspring. Of course, I came across some very wrong ways in my job, but the majority of us are doing our best to create happy, safe environments for our little ones to grow up in. So, continue to do your best and take time to enjoy their childhood because, as we all know, it passes by far too quickly.

Finally, I would like to return to the infamous having-it-all debate, briefly touched on in Chapter 2, in terms of its potential to exacerbate our guilt. For most of the Noughties, every female commentator seemed to be expressing an opinion on how glass ceilings were being broken and women were finally achieving their holy grail of being able to 'have it all'.

It's a discussion I frequently had with the women in my organisation who saw me working in a senior position at the same time as being a single mother to two children. If I'm honest, I felt some internal pressure to say that it was possible to achieve this without any great emotional impact, in an effort to encourage more women to follow me up the ladder. The reality, though, is that it was often very difficult, and sacrifices were made. The trick is to ensure that, in the main, you are prepared to make those compromises without compromising your values. I know how important my financial independence is to me and how doing my job was a part of who I was, and I am happy to acknowledge that. Yes, I did cry in the bath some evenings; I did wonder, on occasions, if I was doing the right thing, but if I had my time again, would I do anything differently? No, probably not.

It might have felt a little easier if I'd had a wife at home, like many of my male colleagues did, as they didn't appear to have to worry about their children turning up on a non-uniform day in school uniform instead of home clothes. Yes, I managed that one too, but Grandpa sorted it out and they were only a few minutes late, although they still claim to have been scarred for life by the experience. If only I had discovered the merits of my multi-colour-coded calendar in those days. If that doesn't mean anything to you, you are going to have to go back to Chapter 4; do not pass Go; do not collect £200!

The reality, of course, was that I usually forgot to check the calendar that everything was written down on anyway. I'm sure my survival at work was directly attributable to my amazing personal assistant. I just needed one at home (as well as one of those wives).

So, accept guilt as a normal emotion, and do all you can to lessen the impact on you and your family.

Success snippet: Don't do guilt.

CHAPTER 6

Role models and mentors

"Tell me and I forget, teach me and I may remember, involve me and I learn" – Benjamin Franklin

I've talked a lot about seeking help in this book, and for me there is no better way to help someone than to be a mentor. Let's start by understanding what we mean by the various terms used to describe offering help and support to others.

A mentor is a trusted counsellor, guide, tutor or coach. This is someone who assists others by sharing their experiences, usually in a one-to-one work environment and with a less experienced colleague. It tends to be an ongoing relationship, and usually relates to personal development in the workplace.

To that end, there should be a joint agreement that the mentor and mentee understand and sign up to. It may be easy to identify a 'role model' in your organisation and seek to have them as a mentor. For mentoring to be successful, however, there needs to be a trusted relationship and a connection between those taking part. We usually choose to be a mentor, but may not see ourselves as a role model.

A role model is a person whose behaviour in a particular role is imitated by others. You can, therefore, have role models in many areas of your life; people whom you aspire to be like, but whom you need not necessarily know at all.

As a role model you might say: "This is the way I work and live my life, which you may want to imitate." But as a mentor you would say: "This is the way I work and live my life, which you may want to imitate, so here are the details of how I have done these things."

Of course, if you are one of a small number of senior women in an organisation, regardless of how you feel, others who wish to achieve a similar position may view you as a role model. This could result in you feeling under pressure if others are making it clear they want to emulate your personal style.

This leaves coaching, which is fast becoming a growing industry, with many individuals and organisations now recognising the huge benefits of having a coach for particular work situations. There's the key difference: coaching is aimed at specific situations or areas for development, and is a relatively short-term activity with the emphasis on performance at work, although personal issues may be discussed.

I have conducted a significant number of coaching conversations with men and women targeting forthcoming interview situations, and for many this involved just one meeting.

So, should you bother going to the effort of finding support to help you achieve your goals at work, or even outside of work? Well, assuming you have identified your goals (don't worry if you haven't; that's the next chapter), it helps to have someone to hold you accountable for the decisions that you have made and help establish the next steps you need to take. It reinforces that you are taking charge of the situation and not just leaving everything in the lap of the gods.

If anyone out there has ever achieved success

through the many weight-loss programmes that require you to attend regular meetings, then I'm sure you'll recognise the benefit of being held to account, and the resulting additional effort that the process encourages. (If, as in my case, it's only on the night before the meeting that you remember the rules, you are obviously unlikely to achieve long-term success.)

Adopting this type of accountable approach to your career goals usually means that you are prepared to make choices, step out of your comfort zone and aim high.

So, let's assume you have identified the person who you want to be your mentor; you have asked for their support and they have agreed. What is going to make that relationship work? Similarly, if someone has chosen you as a mentor and this is your first foray into helping another, here are my 10 top tips for a successful mentoring relationship:

i. Utilise any networking opportunity to choose your mentor. Consider what types of situations might allow you to identify a suitable mentor; perhaps professional association meetings or business networks, as well as opportunities within your own company.

ii. Make sure you both know why you are meeting. As the mentee, are you looking for someone with similar skills to you, or someone who can coach you to develop skills?

iii. Ensure there are clear goals for this relationship that are understood on both sides. These must be agreed in the first meeting to avoid the conversation degenerating into gossip, or time drifting on without achieving anything meaningful.

iv. Don't assume that you are allowed only one mentor. You can have a number of mentors if you are seeking to develop different areas of your life.

v. Establish communication methods and frequency of meetings. You don't always have to meet face to face. Telephone and email communication can be just as effective on some occasions.

vi. Take your time to build trust. Avoid not following through on advice given by the mentor and accepted by you, and try not to cancel meetings at the last minute.

vii. Listen to advice, even if critical. If you receive feedback from your mentor suggesting improvements, try not to react defensively.

viii. Be aware of time limitations. As a mentee, don't be demanding of your mentor's time. As a mentor, don't overstretch yourself; be able to say 'no' assertively.

ix. Say thank you. The mentor is probably sacrificing other opportunities to support you, so make sure you demonstrate that you appreciate the effort they are putting in to your development.

x. Do things differently. Take the opportunity to share your knowledge and experience in different ways. It may be possible for the mentee to shadow the mentor in the workplace, or for you to attend meetings together.

I was extremely fortunate to have the benefit of joining a formal mentoring scheme in the police service. Nationally, female chief officers had set up a scheme where newly promoted superintendents were offered the opportunity to join the scheme and given the choice of a mentor from another force area.

I chose a mentor who lived and worked in an adjoining force and had considerable experience of my business area of criminal justice. We met up every couple of months in the cafe of a garden centre midway between our homes.

We always had a set agenda – well, Caroline did, which was just as well, as my dieting habit of not checking my set targets from the previous meeting until the night before, seemed to have transferred across to these meetings. In fact, the actual dietary targets were not helped by the wide choice of cake available in said cafe! I should add that I did eventually begin to recognise the benefit of implementing Caroline's advice on a daily basis, and not just the night before our next meeting.

We became firm friends and still have those coaching conversations, as she 're-directed' a few years before I did, and so now has different wisdom to pass on. Coffee and cake have also graduated to full-blown lunches with perhaps a small amount of gossip included. This is allowed, as long as business is conducted first.

I have had the privilege of mentoring many women and men over the years, and can truthfully say that, other than watching your own children grow, little else is more satisfying than developing the people around you and observing from the sideline as they achieve their goals.

As I said earlier, success attracts success, so identify and mix with successful people. Okay, so maybe you can't call up Alan Sugar and invite him to join you for a pint in the local, but can you find someone in your organisation that would be prepared to help you achieve your goals? There are few things more beneficial than having a champion to cheer you on; someone who can share their contacts and personal stories with you, and give you an insight into the reality of the challenges they have faced. Be active in identifying someone to be your champion. Face your fear and ask for help; you never know, they might just say yes, and where might that lead?

Now to address another issue for many women: use of the 'ambition' word. Despite there being increasing numbers of successful women in business, politics and the media, to label a woman ambitious is somehow still a slur. In men, it's a trait to be admired, but unless you are an Olympic athlete, as a woman it feels like it has connotations of walking over the opposition in your Prada heels.

Men don't appear to have a problem owning their victories, but women usually seek to explain theirs away by suggesting that it might be luck, or as a result of the work of everyone else. This tendency can also be linked to an inability to accept compliments easily. Does this sound familiar?

Woman to female friend: "I love that skirt; it looks great on you."

Female friend, in self-deprecating voice: "Oh, this old thing? I've had it ages." It might sound like a cliché, but this response is all too common.

This is one area, I am happy to announce, in

which I have made great strides with regard to my daughters. They are particularly astute at accepting compliments graciously, which is far more pleasant for those issuing the compliments with sincerity, and a big step on the way to increasing self-esteem. I am still working on some of their friends, though (and their friends' mothers, too).

Can I suggest, then, that we start a movement to recognise ambition in women as a desire to do well, and accept recognition for our achievements, understanding that this does not mean doing all of this at the cost of those around us. Let's start using the word openly and proudly, and not feel shy about wanting to progress. Surely this is what we want for our daughters (and sons) when we encourage them to work hard at school?

As for being a role model, they have a very different stance, and to me this is when you look to others whom you admire for inspiration and their personal view of the world.

My focus was to be a good role model to my children and show them that life is full of opportunities, but I soon became aware that other women at work often saw me as a role model. This was not something I had set out to become, but it turned out to be something that I took very seriously, wanting other women to see the available opportunities and reach out for them. I strongly believe that those of us in positions of influence should do just that. For women, it is even more important, as it is often by watching others that we start to believe we too can achieve such things. I have taken inspiration from some great women in my time; some of whom I have observed from afar; others I have had the advantage of knowing well, and who have made me want to strive to be a better leader.

So, what advice did I give other women in the organisation who came to me for that support? It was important for me to have reached a professional position of influence at the time of becoming a mother, as it gave me greater flexibility, although it inevitably carried additional pressures. So, I say don't back down too prematurely when planning that next promotion or job application, take opportunities as they arise, and give yourself the chance to make choices further down the line. The downside of this strategy is that you leave yourself open to becoming 'the oldest mum in the school'. (I still won at sports' day, though!)

Success snippet: Receiving support isn't a sign of weakness.

CHAPTER 7

8 steps to unlocking your true potential

"Human beings the world over need freedom and security that they may be able to realise their full potential" – *Aung San Suu Kyi*

So far, we have created a framework by which you can check your progress and help build success into your chosen path. This chapter will assist you in checking that the path you have chosen is the right one for you. At this point I should emphasise that reaching the top in your current or any future organisation is not the only measure of success at work.

Step one: Identify *your* true potential.

True or full potential will not mean the same for everyone, and certainly does not always involve fighting your way through glass ceilings or indeed over glass cliffs.

Although I have written this book to help those that seek success and at the same time may have to juggle home and work demands, it does not necessarily follow that your ultimate dream takes you in that direction. I do, however, want you to be aware of how much you are capable of achieving should you set your mind to it and then choose to follow that path with a plan.

Interestingly, I did not set out to reach the rank of chief superintendent in the police service when I left school. In fact, it was a great disappointment to my poor mum when, having been to a private school until the age of 11, securing a place at the local girls' grammar school and then failing my A levels, I announced that I was going to work full time in Etam, where I had been working on Saturdays. For those of you too young to remember this iconic brand, think New Look. Well, all credit to Mum, she came down and met the manageress and, true to my word, I proceeded to spend my days straightening skirt hems and shirtsleeves. In fact, I still can't abide clothes in a wardrobe not all facing the same way and in graduated lengths, but less of my clothing obsessions.

Within 18 months, I was the assistant manager at a local branch and also had a Saturday job in a nearby department store, so I suppose the drive to achieve was there from an early age.

Soon after this promotion, I was persuaded to change course, and moved full time to a local restaurant where I had been working in the evenings, while still at Etam. I soon discovered that this meant I could no longer go out to night clubs with my friends because I was working in the restaurant at night, so this was consequently followed by spells in the civil service (a proper job), before leaving to become the first female sales representative to sell knitting wool into local wool shops. Yes, wool shops really were in every town and city, and I thought it bizarre that there were no other women selling in that industry, given it was such a popular 'female' hobby at the time. I soon realised that most of the lovely ladies running the shops actually looked forward to meeting all of those charming, young, male sales assistants with their boxes of samples!

To begin with, it was quite a novelty, and I genuinely enjoyed driving along the pretty roads of

Devon and Cornwall. Sadly, my boss eventually managed to persuade a top salesman from a rival company to join us, and he brought his loyal clients in Devon and Cornwall with him. This meant I headed off to the wilds of Berkshire, Buckinghamshire and Oxfordshire to sell my wares, and I have to tell you that the good ladies of those counties are far more likely to buy their clothes than knit them!

Very soon, another opportunity arose out of a chance conversation with the owner of a knitting and sewing-machine shop, the outcome being that I became the shop manager and spent many hours making things for my stall at a local market, while earning a good wage. At that time, my main ambition was to open a button shop with a friend – yes, there really were shops that just sold buttons, too. Well, in addition to a few other haberdashery supplies.

During all of these career changes, which occurred within a six-year period, my parents were only ever supportive of my diverse career choices. It became clear to them that I was doing things that I really enjoyed, and doing them well. It may not have been their ideal, but they never let that show; they had always brought me up to believe that I could do anything I wanted, and I certainly turned my hand to quite a few different things in an effort to prove that point.

It was at this stage that I decided to apply to join

the local police force, based on my belief that I could then leave my boyfriend at the time, as I would have to move away. I am sure my parents were thrilled at the prospect of an even more 'proper' job, and as it turned out I didn't move away!

My advice, then, is to seek as much support as you can from those around you, and follow your passion wherever it may take you.

Over many years, I have had conversations with women who have told me how unhappy they are in their current jobs, but that they have no idea what else they could do.

One of the best ways of identifying what could fulfil you is to think of the occasions when you have been so occupied in an activity that you lose all track of time; or when you feel a true sense of purpose from a project you are undertaking. Is that something you could make a living from, or develop further in order to eventually make it pay sufficiently well?

I have a friend who makes the most incredible cakes for, until recently, only family and friends, refusing to take any money for them. Gradually, over a period of time, she has acknowledged that people will indeed pay for these delicious creations, and started planning how this could become a future career. Her personal circumstances mean that she currently cannot walk away from her well-paid sales job, but she has secured a more flexible working arrangement that means she can start to build up a client base, and I am certain that one day she will step away from her day job and begin fulfilling her true potential.

I realise that this step is not as straightforward for everyone, and many people are insistent that it is impossible to leave their well-paid jobs as they support a certain lifestyle for them and their family. The reality, however, is that if your job is making you incredibly unhappy, that will already be impacting upon those around you, and perhaps an honest conversation as a family will bring up some opposing views on what is more important to each of you.

As alluded to earlier, if this were your last day on the planet, would your review of your life to date be satisfying?

Discover the dream, career change or new goal that you are going to work towards and which will unlock your potential.

Step two: Believe in your own abilities and get started.

Right, you have identified your dream job and now you need to make sure that you truly believe in your ability to secure it. As you start to take steps towards your goal, you will develop the confidence to keep going, but taking that first step, which is likely to be the hardest and is also likely to involve you stepping out of your comfort zone, can be very scary.

Getting started is often the key. I'm as good as the next person at procrastinating and finding excuses not to start something, especially if it is going to be a challenge. This is very common, and an issue that can intensify any initial lack of confidence in our abilities. It's like that nagging, negative voice I was talking about earlier. All the other, often more menial jobs that need to be done hover over us while we do anything else but tackle them. Eventually, it gets to the point where we feel completely overwhelmed and convinced we cannot achieve anything; certainly not our dream.

The trick is to make a list. No, not the usual short list of big projects that need heaps of money and probably planning permission to achieve. I want you to make a list of *all* the jobs that you need to do. Write them down now, on the blank notes pages at the back of this book. If you are a smartphone tech, make a list using one of those special 'apps'. Right, I'm going to make a coffee while you do that…

Okay, now I want you to identify just one simple thing on the list that you can do immediately. If not straightaway, within a day or so, and do it! I promise that completion of this task will make you feel better about yourself; it might even make you feel the need to do another and then another. I should, at this point, probably confess to the occasional, slight amendment when using this technique: adding recently completed tasks to my list and then crossing them off. I know, I'm only cheating myself, but somehow it kick-starts me.

Once your head is clear of all those demands, you can begin to think clearer about that goal, and often this exercise will serve to help you realise that many of those jobs you have listed are either not that important, or could be done just as well by others around you.

So, what is the answer to procrastination? Just do it!

It is also important to realise that our goals can change over time. We change, circumstances change, and others around us change, so our goals should be flexible too. They needn't be set in stone; you are allowed to make adjustments as you go along, providing that you don't use this as an excuse to stop trying to reach them.

When you are truly committed to your new goal, you will be passionate about it and, with your newfound confidence and increased self-esteem, genuinely believe that you can achieve it.

Remind yourself regularly that you are good enough to do this.

Step three: Take small steps and aim high.

When we are totally focused on striving for our goals, the outcome can be that we get carried away with concentrating on the ultimate dream and, as a result, become disillusioned when it doesn't materialise immediately.

My father and I have a shared saying: "If you can't finish it by lunchtime, don't bother starting it." Mind you, he is so fixated on the limited amount of time that he has left that he refuses to buy a large tube of toothpaste in case he shuffles off this mortal coil before he gets a chance to use it all.

The need to finish by lunchtime probably has something to do with the fact that we both become distracted very easily. It is no good suggesting that I help de-clutter a room; the first drawer and I'm on the floor planning my new scrapbooking hobby, wondering where those two hours went.

It also reinforces the need to see results quickly to maintain motivation, so if this applies to you, it will probably be more beneficial to break down that goal into smaller, more easily achievable steps.

As another favourite saying goes, you can't eat an elephant in one bite, so the trick is to identify the mini goals that support your long-term goal, and follow a plan to achieve all of them. (Why do they say that about elephants?)

Here we go then; grab a pen and some paper, or the notes app on your phone, and start to create a map of the steps needed to achieve your goal:

In the centre of the page, write down in large letters your ultimate dream/goal, with a realistic date for when you want to achieve it, and then draw a circle around it. (You'll probably need quite a sophisticated app for that bit.)

From this central theme, start to create 'branches' by writing down those mini goals that will support your ultimate goal, making sure that they can be easily accomplished, and as you complete each one, you will be one more step closer to your ultimate goal. (There are mind-map apps for this. I've downloaded them, but still prefer my pretty book – don't tell him indoors.)

If there are obstacles in your way, document them, along with creative ways to overcome them. (Extra work needed here; don't gloss over that.)

If you realise that you are going to need help from others to achieve some of your mini goals, write down the names of those you will ask to help you. (Preferably, add a date of when you are going to ask them by.)

The more steps you have, the easier it will be to

achieve, and if you can find a way to create *daily* actions or steps, the more likely you are to be successful.

Each time you achieve one of your mini goals, you will build your confidence and commitment, and this is vital if you are to reach that long-term goal. This way you can make even the most challenging goal achievable.

When you get used to stepping out of that comfort zone, you start to challenge yourself more often, and very soon almost anything seems achievable. Like most things, practice turns this newly acquired skill into a habit. You really can aim high, dream big and go for it. As that famous sports brand would say: Just do it.

Be confident and reach for the stars.

Step four: Be courageous in your beliefs, and own your feelings.

So, with all this enthusiasm, energy and positivity going for us, it should be relatively easy to achieve that dream. Of course, if it were as straightforward as that, we would probably all be extremely happy, healthy, high achievers; but so often, internal beliefs can limit what we set out to do.

These beliefs start forming at a very early age, and are influenced by much of what is around us, whether that's our parents, siblings, school teachers or whoever. These beliefs often sit in our subconscious, yet can still affect much of what we do for years to come.

If, like me, you were brought up to believe that you could have a go at almost anything, that is likely to be your continued outlook on life – in my case often without thought of any of the possible consequences. In the main, this attitude builds a positive self-belief. If, however, you were brought up like a friend of mine, in the shadow of an elder sibling with huge comparisons between them of their school results and other achievements, then you could well end up internalising feelings of inferiority, believing that you are no good at anything and, as a consequence, set your ambitions pretty low. In the face of such limiting beliefs, it can take great courage to stand up for what you believe and aim high.

For some people, the first step in striving for a dream is to actually allow themselves to consider it possible, even inside their own head. A far bigger step would be to articulate that thought.

Courage, therefore, means different things to different people; for some, getting through each day takes great personal courage, while others have days filled with great opportunities that they grab with both hands.

Courage comes from facing and overcoming fears (we have talked about that already). It builds your confidence and encourages you to take risks. It involves doing the sort of things that successful entrepreneurs do all the time.

The co-founders of Google spent years trying to get anyone who would listen to invest in their idea of a dedicated search company. I imagine their passion and belief kept them going, despite the views of many who thought their idea was ridiculous.

To succeed when following your dream may well mean confronting others who think that you can't succeed, but take inspiration from all those who have overcome adversity, such as Thomas Edison, who tried more than a thousand times to create the light bulb. Fortunately for us, he didn't give up, and stuck to his beliefs.

Courage is being afraid, but carrying on anyway.

The second half of this step is recognising the importance of owning your feelings. Learning to master our emotions is a step towards preventing them from mastering us. We talked earlier about the benefits of emotional intelligence and being aware of the emotions of others. Aristotle is quoted as saying: "Anybody can become angry – that is easy, but to be angry with the right person and to the right degree and at the right time and for the right purpose, and in the right way – that is not within everybody's power and is not easy."

We all make a choice when reacting to situations, and the response of "you make me so…" is familiar to many of us when someone has acted in a way that results in us feeling happy or perhaps angry or upset. The moment we give the other person the power to make us feel a particular way, we risk making a victim of ourselves and becoming powerless.

A simple change of language to "I feel…" gives the power back to you and, even if the feeling is distressing, it can be far less scary if you recognise that it is the feeling you are owning. Although I have recommended that you face those fears, just acknowledging that they are a bit frightening can make them far more easy to deal with, rather than attempting to charge on through, pretending that the situation is a piece of cake.

I challenge you to practice this choice of language on your children – mine have sussed my attempts at this and often withdraw from arguments saying: "You've got that quiet, serious voice on again." If nothing else, that voice is far better than the screeching one.

As soon as you own your own feelings, you realise you are not responsible for the feelings of others.

Step five: Accept that setbacks will happen, but remain positive.

I spoke earlier of failing brilliantly; taking setbacks in your stride and recognising that they can be an important lesson in life; a way of finding out what works and what doesn't.

Research has proved that if you expect mistakes, not in a negative "whatever I do, I will fail" mindset, but with a calm accepting "things will not always go my way" philosophy, you are more likely to be successful.

The late nineteenth-century philosopher Friedrich Nietzsche is often credited with saying that what doesn't kill you makes you stronger – surprisingly not originating from the Kelly Clarkson song. He actually wrote: "That which does not kill us makes us stronger," but the sentiment is the same. In fact, studies of trauma survivors have shown that some report positive changes and enhanced personal development following the trauma they have survived. The phenomenon has been called post-traumatic growth, and refers to any positive change experienced as a result of a major life crisis or traumatic event.

I am not, of course, suggesting that we actively go out and seek traumatic situations, but just that it is worth remembering that when life sends those trucks headlong toward us and we do finally reach the other side of the situation, we may well end up feeling a much stronger person.

I certainly wouldn't recommend divorce when you have two three-year-olds to bring up, at the same time as holding down a challenging job, but there is no doubt that this experience made me a stronger and ultimately happier person; one who is now rarely put off by run-of-the-mill challenges.

Try not to wallow for too long in the misery of the moment; just move on to the next phase, knowing that you will be better for the change of direction. Don't see setbacks as failures to throw you off course, but rather view them as useful lessons for the future and opportunities for personal growth.

Step six: Get help and be inspired.

Now it is time to put into action the advice from the last chapter. Who is going to give you support to achieve your dream? Have you identified the person who will help you take the next steps, and who will be your mentor or coach?

It may be that achieving your chosen dream would require you to leave your current job, therefore seeking support within your workplace to achieve this may not be the best way forward.

Consider using the services of a professional

coach or mentor, either through word of mouth or via the internet. Think of it as an investment in your future and, if necessary, be prepared to pay for that advice. I know a number of people who will happily throw money at a gym membership that they never use, but seem to think that a similar monthly cost for coaching assistance is completely unjustifiable.

If finances are difficult, consider other opportunities, perhaps through group sessions or buying a book to learn from, not forgetting libraries, other resource centres and the world wide web.

Who is going to be your goal buddy? If you have a shared dream with someone else, like my friend and I had with the button shop, then you can give encouragement to each other, but be sure your plan is shared as well as the work to achieve it.

Do you have friends who have similar plans or ideas? Could you spend an evening together writing, drawing, designing or just getting inspiration from each other?

It is also really important to make sure you receive help in terms of business advice if you don't know anything about accounting, business planning, marketing or PR. Consider the investment in professional skills early on to avoid expensive mistakes later.

How are other people going to help you on the road to achieving your goals?

Look for inspiration in all sorts of places and keep a notebook with you to jot down those ideas. (My husband will be baulking at this notion, as there must be another app specifically designed to record inspirations.)

Make some of your mini goals fun in order to ease the pressure. If you are trying to write, take time off and go to a theme park with the kids, even if, like me, you spend most of your time in the coffee shop because you're too scared to tackle the rides. (Those are the fears I have chosen not to face and it is quite easy to set the laptop up and crack on.)

Make sure you have a clear vision of what success looks like. It often helps to write it down in detail or draw a picture of what life will be like when you've reached that goal. Think about what it will be like in a month, a year and five years when you have achieved that goal.

Visualise exactly how it will feel.

Step seven: Enjoy the moment and appreciate everything.

Remember my friend stopping her car to look at the rainbow? This is the step that may well be the most difficult to implement when we lead such busy lives. I

read a great article recently that talked about
'busyness' being a badge of honour in the workplace;
a sort of bragging without actually saying: "Look at
how busy and stressed I am; I'm really important and
productive."

Of course, the reality is far from this. Excessive
multitasking means we are likely to be reducing
quality for quantity. Effective output usually requires
focus and concentration, and working without taking
breaks is proven to be ineffective, so the busier we
think we are, the less we will actually get done. If you
feel frantic because your calendar is so full every day,
a solution is to diary in 'empty' slots. I know that this
will seem impossible at the beginning, but actually
taking the time to sit, breathe, think and look around
you can bring real benefits to the way you feel.
Depending on the culture in your workplace, you may
have to invent a cover story for this time slot.

I have made a conscious effort to be relaxed
when waiting in queues; I have even let people
through ahead of me, and I have to tell you that in
terms of spreading feelings of calm, it makes a real
difference. It also gives you an opportunity to look
around and observe what else is happening in the
world. So, while I am still not a big fan of queuing, I
no longer huff and puff at the trainee checkout
operator, or the elderly lady who has forgotten her tin
of polish and gone off in search of it, leaving us all

stuck in her wake. I even take the opportunity to chat to strangers and leaf through magazines!

This is a great quote from the actor Sid Caesar: "In between goals is a thing called life, that has to be lived and enjoyed."

So, while I am explaining the steps to help you achieve your goals, this should not be to the detriment of the rest of your life. Make sure you know what is happening here and now, and enjoy the present.

Stop the car, get out and enjoy that rainbow. Give yourself rewards as you go along, appreciate the journey and recognise your achievements, but more of that later!

Step eight: Never give up!

Not giving up is probably the hardest of all the steps, but none of the others will work if you do not commit to forging ahead with your goal. The easier thing to do is give up and, as I have said before, this is what is going to mark you out as different from everyone else – you will keep going and you will not give up!

It is difficult to keep going when success seems to be a long way off, but that is why we have the smaller, mini goals. They are easier to achieve and each small success grows your confidence and belief in your ability to reach your ultimate goal. The most common reason for people giving up is that the road ahead seems so long and difficult to navigate. If you set yourself a target to run a marathon in 12 months, it is a rather daunting commitment, but if broken down into a couple of miles a month, those smaller chunks suddenly become more achievable.

Sometimes, when you are reaching these smaller milestones, other setbacks will still throw you off course, so one of the best ways to stay on track is by involving others, whether as buddies or just to keep you accountable.

Very early on in the decision to write this book, I started to tell people around me about my plans, because I knew that this would keep me motivated. The more people I told, the more I felt committed to carrying on and finishing it rather than having to admit I couldn't do it, which probably says a lot about my drive to achieve my goals.

I wonder if JK Rowling ever thought about giving up when 12 publishers turned her down? The reality is that if you give up on your dreams, they will surely die, but if you want to make them come true, focus your free time on following your plan and working your socks off!

Success snippet: No matter how long it takes, keep chasing those dreams and make them your reality.

CHAPTER 8

Celebrate success

"Celebrate your small successes on the way to great ones"
— Gill Donnell

So, here we are at the central theme of this book: the importance of celebrating your successes.

I have talked a lot about slowing down and enjoying what is taking place around you, being present for yourself and others, in effect celebrating the experiences of life. The danger of focusing solely on achieving our goals is that we forget the other lessons and end up chasing perfection again, pushing ourselves harder and harder.

The message of this book is, therefore, to understand what it is that you want from life, believe that you can achieve it, but in doing so, don't get sucked into a cycle of constant striving.

We have already established that women tend towards the 'perfect' gene, constantly striving to do better, because their normal way is just not good enough. If behaving like this makes you think there's no time to slow down, to reflect on what you have achieved – or perhaps you don't even accept the possibility that you might have achieved anything – then you really need to stop now. Step back and smell the roses, coffee or whatever else it is that you enjoy smelling. Perhaps stop to make a drink and consider re-reading the earlier chapters, unless of course you have skipped straight to this chapter, in which case you probably do need to go back and face the stuff at the start!

In the main, as a society, we tend to focus our celebrations on significant events, such as birthdays, anniversaries, Valentine's Day or similar, and not on life in general. Now that we are becoming more used to slowing down and being aware of what is around us, we also need to make sure we acknowledge reaching each of those milestones on the way towards our ultimate goals.

The key here is to get used to celebrating achievements, however small, and it's good to start the process by writing up a list of what you have already accomplished, so that you concentrate on the positives, rather than beat yourself up about the jobs that you haven't managed to complete yet.

For some people, finishing work on time could be quite significant, while for others, putting on trainers and jogging to the postbox could be that first small step that turns into running a 10k race six months later.

I wouldn't recommend missing out the mini goals, as I did a couple of years ago when I took on the challenge to complete a sponsored race. This is how it went:

- Signed the forms for the seafront 10k (goal)

- Raised sponsorship (commitment)

- Was dragged around the course – the seafront at Bournemouth in my case, although it felt like I was running to Brighton (support)

- Jogged/ran/walked/crawled with two 'proper runners' – they were forced to bully me to the finish line (role models)

- I made it! (achievement)

- In the euphoria of the post-run champagne, (celebrate success) I swore through the hyperventilation, never again without proper training

I definitely should have set myself some small steps over a decent period of training time, but in reality, I feared the energy and enthusiasm might wear off, as running is not my exercise of choice. Actually, other than walking my little dog, I am not sure I have an exercise of choice.

Now I am off for yet another coffee (I think I may have to set a goal to reduce my coffee consumption), so write down your list of achievements below. Really push yourself if you find it difficult, and write down five achievements from the last couple of days that you can celebrate, and I refuse to believe that you have not achieved anything in that period of time.

To help the process, I have written down my five latest achievements for you, and note that this does not have to be about climbing Kilimanjaro yet, although I now know an amazing number of women who have done just that through adopting this process.

Gill's five most recent achievements:

i.   I walked the dog twice in one day. (Poor thing is exhausted.)

ii.   I cooked four different dishes from scratch (At the same time.)

iii.   I finished the previous chapter of this book (Yippee!)

iv.   I actually rang the taxman about my change of details (Two months late, but hey.)

v.   I made sure the girls stuck to their revision timetables. (Instead of letting them watch trashy TV.)

Write down your five in the space below:

i.   ....

ii.   ....

iii.   ....

iv.   ....

v.   ....

I hope that doing that exercise has helped you to keep focus on the positive progress you are making, and if you found it easy then great, but my experience of the many women whom I have encouraged to undertake this activity is that their initial response is: "Oh no, I haven't achieved anything."

There is no doubt that when it comes to recognising our own achievements in life, practice makes perfect – yes, I know we said excellent will do, but this is different.

If you drive a car, do you have to think in detail about every gear change and turn of the wheel? Could you read a book on driving and be able to get in a car and drive? No, we need to practise, but very soon it becomes second nature (although the odd scrape still somehow gets onto my car's bodywork).

Once you have mastered the ability to recognise and celebrate your achievements, however small, it can be really beneficial to keep a record of them and update it regularly. I have a gorgeous journal that a friend of mine bought me. Each page is different and it cries out to be filled in using copperplate handwriting. That bit is unfortunate because my writing is second only to that of my doctor, but nevertheless, I like to focus on making it neat and legible. I keep it with me at all times to jot down my inspirations (currently for this book), and at the back it has a list of my goals and also my more significant achievements.

The other benefit to this is that, on days when

things do become overwhelming, or on a day when, as we say in our house, you just feel 'out of sorts', it allows you to look back at how far you have come.

Actually identifying and then writing down achievements can also be a good exercise for teenagers to master when Ms Negative comes knocking at the door, which is far too often for my liking. They will probably require some help to start off, but the long-term benefits can be well worth the effort, as it is a life skill that truly works when tackling future goals.

Don't forget that the benefit of celebrating extends to making sure we celebrate the achievements of others. My mum and dad were great at this when I was growing up, to the point of overdoing it sometimes, but ask my girls – there is nothing better than when, at the age of 15 and feeling like the whole world is against you, Nanny turns up enthusing on how wonderful you look, how clever you are and what delicious cakes you've made. (Even if you did forget the baking powder, she is never going to say so!)

It is a simple yet incredibly powerful act; be appreciative of those around you, especially your children. Tell them when you are proud of them; apart from anything else, it does wonders for their self-esteem, and we know how important that is!

In the same vein, practise gratitude. There is a real groundswell of opinion about the huge health benefits of this. Type 'benefits of gratitude' into your favourite search engine and you will be amazed at the blogs, courses and numerous books that advocate this simple approach to life. It is very difficult, if you make a habit of reflecting on what you have to be grateful for, to be anything other than positive about life and those around you. It certainly makes you more appreciative and likely to be less self-centred and materialistic, and it works wonders for your self-esteem.

So, be prepared to celebrate your successes, no matter what they are, and your wildest dreams will not be out of your reach. Each time that you achieve one of your mini goals, celebrate that achievement and set a new goal on your road to success. A celebration is essential to keeping you inspired, whether it is going out for dinner, having a facial or buying those fabulous shoes that you've been wanting for a while (another weakness of mine). The way you celebrate doesn't matter; the main thing is that you reward yourself for your hard work, dedication and success in achieving the target.

Once you have achieved your goal, go back and assess what worked, what didn't and what you could have done differently. This evaluation is key when tackling business or career goals, as often we set a variety of short and mid-term goals, and can get caught up in slavishly following our original plans. Times and lives change, as do priorities, and you must make sure that the goal you are currently working on fits into the way you want to live your life.

A final tip worth repeating: if you are a young woman setting off down your chosen career path, don't make career choices too early, especially if getting married and having children is one of your life aims. I have seen a number of young women start to almost 'wind down' their career aspirations on the basis that at some point in the future they are likely to want to work part time. I never gave that much thought while I achieved my various promotions and, as I said earlier, I was quite senior in my organisation by the time I had my girls, so was able to work flexibly to the benefit of both myself and my employer. Of course, I would not recommend nor dissuade anyone from starting a family at the age of 40, but if you do, it might be worth taking out insurance against having twins, as the likelihood of that happening is apparently greater as you get older!

So, don't forget to celebrate those achievements. And then get ready for your next challenge…

Affirmation: I am worthy of success.

WHAT NEXT?

I hope you have enjoyed this book, but mostly that it has inspired you to reach for your goals and become used to celebrating both your own achievements and those of others.

As a result of researching and writing down my thoughts on the subject of the personal development of women, I have become particularly enthusiastic about doing all I can to make sure that the next generation of young women are helped along in the amazing journey that life has to offer.

When I think back to the number of women who have taken part in the Springboard personal-development courses we have run over the years and who said they wished they had had a similar opportunity 20 years previously, it makes my desire to 'get the message out there' even greater.

So, do spread the word, and encourage others to challenge themselves and take opportunities along the way. If you are a mum/sister/aunt/grandmother or another role model to young girls, please demonstrate a positive approach to life and work, and at the same time raise your own self-esteem.

Don't let this be the end of your journey; continue to network and seek out people who can help you in your goals, and help others as much as you can.

I have provided a source of further reading at the end of this book (just before those useful notes pages) and also included websites and podcasts that I find beneficial.

If you would like to know more about my work, visit my website, which is dedicated to developing the potential of women and girls:
www.successfulwomen.training

Follow me on Twitter: **@SuccessWomenTng**

Visit my Facebook page: **SuccessfulWomen.Training**

If you would like to contact me or receive further details of the courses that I offer, please visit the website or email me at:
gill@successfulwomen.training

USEFUL RESOURCES

www.dove.co.uk/en/Our-Mission/Dove-Self-Esteem-Project-Get-Involved/

Great online resources for parents, teachers and individuals.

www.springboardconsultancy.com

Full details of the international personal and work development training company.

www.artofbrilliance.co.uk

Links to books, podcasts and free resources from the 'brilliant' Andy Cope and his positive psychology philosophy.

www.nourishlifecoaching.com

Find my favourite life-coaching podcasts – *The Bright Side* broadcast on an American radio show.

www.thesumoguy.com

Website for Paul McGee, I highly recommend his book S.U.M.O. (shut up and move on).

www.authentichappiness.sas.upenn.edu

The website of the Positive Psychology Center at the University of Pennsylvania, which focuses on the study of such things as positive emotions, strengths-based character and healthy institutions. It has some great free questionnaires you can access.

www.bis.gov.uk//assets/biscore/business-law/docs/w/11-745-women-on-boards.pdf

Lord Davies' independent review into women on boards, published in February 2011, stated that at the current rate of change it will take over 70 years to achieve gender-balanced boardrooms in the UK.

ABOUT THE AUTHOR

Gill is an experienced leader, motivational speaker and coach, who has spent much of her working life promoting the role of women in the workplace and supporting individuals to achieve their full potential.

As a speaker, Gill uses life experiences and humorous stories to inform her audiences.

Many of the women who have attended her development courses over the years have talked about it as a life-changing experience.

Having spent time as a successful female role model in a male-dominated organisation, while being a single mum of twins, Gill is uniquely placed to understand the challenges faced by women in the workplace.

In 2009, Gill's work on women's development was recognised by Her Majesty the Queen with the award of an MBE.

In 2014 Gill set up her company Successful Women, dedicated to offering online and offline support to women, especially those busy working mums and in 2015 she won the Dorset Venus Award for The Most Influential Woman.

<u>NOTES</u>

<u>NOTES</u>

NOTES

54956954R00075

Made in the USA
Charleston, SC
18 April 2016